seula

by stasha ginsburg

Bone Soup Press
Eugene, Oregon

Published by Bone Soup Press
http://stalkingstories.wordpress.com
movingthestory@gmail.com
Copyright © 2015 Stasha Ginsburg

Cover art: Stasha Ginsburg

Published & printed in the United States of America

creativity transforms

TABLE OF CONTENTS

Introduction 7

Songlines

Navigating Foam 10

For the Chamisa 12

Becoming 14

It happened like this 18

A cold poem 20

Just a Hearth 22

Womblines

Birds and the Bees 25

Ode to Passion 28

The raising of the dead 30

becoming mama 32

Mila's poppy 37

becoming mama II 42

Seula 45

Re-wilding

Beneath beneath 50

Re-enchanting the erotic 52

becoming family 55

molt 60

Baubo 61

the call to adventure 65

the call to adventure II 68

what spring said   70

waking inside   72

detours   74

INTRODUCTION

Australian Aborigines say that the big stories—the stories worth telling and retelling, the ones in which you may find the meaning of your life—are forever stalking the right teller, sniffing and tracking like predators hunting their prey in the bush. —Robert Moss, Dreamgates

Poems have always stalked me. They speak from the belly, pelvis, sky, bones, blood, longing, hunger, wolves, waves and beasts. Sometimes they are subtle, quiet and slippery. Most often they rumble and burn consistently true. I also stalk poems. I have found them in between ocean waves, inside dreaming and waking, beneath stones, above clouds, in compost beds, arroyos, black river foam, gnarled oak trees, acorn seeds, foreign streets, the color red, fairytales, maps, boundaries, edges and tide pools.

When I do not pen the poems that rattle my foundation, I am restless, caged and wild with nowhere to roam. Poems bring me back to the wilderness of my psyche and to the underworld netherworld territories that dance within my spirit and soul. Poems bring me back to source, to cosmology, to self and nothing-ness. Poetry is the closest human experience I have with the divine.

I listen to the guardians of language. The muses and the ancient wordsmiths throw poems at me. I catch them. They catch me. They make me, mold me, shape me, eat me, dissolve me, digest me, and empty me. They grow wings on my spine. When they have said what they needed to say, I feel more whole, more human. I feel more rooted. I know myself and my place more and more. I become.

Poetry lives between the worlds. She flows on ancient springs where dragons and roots mingle with fire and ice. She bubbles and she growls. She is fierce and unpredictable. She comes and goes like a mist or prayer, a hailstorm or the sweet branches of willow blowing in the breeze.

In the land of poetry, I die and am reborn. I am caterpillar and cocoon, butterfly and egg. I migrate. The poems move me across time and space. The temporal and ephemeral. Paradox and Balance.

This is a collection of poetry from 2008 to the present. It meanders through place, body, imagination and memory. It can be read from beginning to end, or simply as the muses inspire. Open the book to a random page from time to time. The poem that you open to is food for the soul.

When I was a little girl, I wrote my first collection of poems on the back of my mother's checkbooks. It has been a dream of mine to publish a 'real' collection of poetry since then. I have kept the dream a secret. Finally, the muses told me that they would stop coming if I didn't share the poems I have collected over the last 7 years. They tell me it is not healthy to collect wild animals and keep them secret. They must be seen if they are to breathe and roam.

I. songlines

navigating foam

the foam made it simple. it moved slowly.

there are several ways to see it. his name was puck. it was summer. he was chewing burdock root. he took me to maple creek. that place makes me feel true.

when navigating place it is good to have a guide. puck took me to the valley of the singing frogs. we bowed our heads through old growth trees and skinny arches. puck didn't speak. the day was common. i sneezed. the sun appeared and disappeared. the frogs began singing.

i thought of saturn and time. time with puck isn't straight-up and logical. puck makes it round. my 98 year-old next-door neighbor told me, "i go to maple creek and first thing is i jump over the creek. i fell in once, but no matter. maple creek is my piece of heaven."

the winter teaches how a thing freezes. and how body and place make it come alive again. winter turns to spring. i discover innocence. this is why white trilliums bloom in summer.

the foam is the eye of horus. now it becomes the birth of a star.

we follow foam to boulders. our faces meet wind and waves kiss our cheeks. puck wants us to see the bearded tree. "look," he points —an eagle circles. it becomes the most ordinary thing in the world.

beyond wind is the sound of ocean. at the edge my memory goes backwards to the place where I was born, where ocean waves and shells contain sound like a mother's womb. the river makes foam. the lake makes waves. they don't say anything. the lake tosses water back and forth.

place moves memory through my belly and water through my eyes. here, streets say cerro gordo, gambia oak, and calle pelligroso. they don't say iron, gold, birch or maple. water rushes in the north and i catch my breath. here, wind does that. dry, cracked arroyos announce place. forests and deserts speak differently. the oak tree near the cholla and chamisa speaks a foreign language. my body is an archeologist.

foam moves past trees that crawl through ore-colored stones. i'm in both places simultaneously. i feel like my grandmother's geraniums. i'll grow roots wherever i am. i know the story of where i come from. i know the names of the things that grew around me and what i'm growing towards. i'm curious about what is growing towards me.

the foam is a quilt. it matures, recedes and dissolves. it is place and a black river slowing down from falls to the mouth of lake superior. it is desire and bright blue sky. it is wing and bone-white birch. it is hunger, taste, wild ramps and huckleberries. it is skipping stone, two fishermen and a speedboat. it is soft clay. it brings me here —to hard clay and arroyo and then there, to soft clay and wave.

it reminds me of the boys i went fishing with at age fifteen. they jumped off the bridge and i shrieked. we drank budweiser all day. they pissed in the river. we watched the sunset and became still. rocks, trees, clouds and words grew into me. I forgot and foam moved and reminded me.

i want to grow this way forever. these images clench my belly. i want to remember the words of foam when i am 80. i write because my words are seeds. they cling to my pant legs like burdock thistles. i carry them to dry places. their memory makes me cry. it fertilizes old stories into new patterns.

For the chamisa

I can barely step
without breaking.
It is dry. And then it is soft.
So soft. And the waves come rolling in. Like clouds
they pummel through time.
I feel them approaching from 135 million years
ago. Gravity like this is unbearable.
The story is so much bigger than me.
And then there is sky.
And it is blue like water
and my hands are red like blood.
Waves like this bring me crashing to my knees.

And then there is a crack.
I can see where time teases me.
Calcite lines etched like needle fish on the stones
that know things.
They call me home.

I know now why 'to re-member'
is to put pieces back together.
Yet I continue to break like clay
in hand wet cold with snow.

135-million-years-time descended.
Just like that.
As if it were a dreaming caterpillar and
my pelvis an
open invitation for wings.

My words turn to blood.

It is softer than a womb.
It yellows me from the inside out. It is like fossilized coral.
It is the one-month-left-till-spring chamisa stalks
and I taste kelp.
I don't understand how
the violence of sky passes
or the ways in which shadows dance.
They tell different stories while the wind is still.
And someone said that knowing too much can cause a person to
feel old too soon.

I understand why the tree bore fruit
and why I had to taste it on my lips
and why this made me fall.

I stepped into the shadows
where the snakes hide.
I made this round globe of mud
wet from tears.
I put it here and I said
apple.
Body.
And then I said earth.
And then it said nothing.

I smeared on my face
these paprika red hands.

And the magpie laughed.
And the bone shard taught me
the eternity of death
and the shell of an ancient sea
said nothing more than circles within circles of time.

The violence of blood spilled between my legs.
It was nothing like what I thought.
It came earlier with the passing eclipse of a moon.
It was a different sort of birth.
It carved tears out of stone.
They melted ice.
And life came to be
in a dry ancient sea.

Becoming

Can't sleep.
The moon speaks.
Night awakens me
 Gives me life.
 The darkness feels so alive.

I am night.
I am a sheath
        covering this body that
        I am becoming into more and more.
        Night that I am gives me more stars
        gives me more suns
        gives me more colors.
        In black or white I discover a millennium
        that I am, this evening song.

My identity disappears.
        I lose what I wasn't
        and do not yet know this how.
        I empty.
        I breathe.
        I know
        that nothing
        enters from a broken door.
        I am the door
        and the crack
        and this black, thick time awakening.
        I am bat wings dancing.
        I am that bat
        that fear
        that bear
        that cave
        the hiding place.
        I am the darkened folds of leaves.
        I am the soil beneath me
        the nutrients
        descending into seeds dreaming
        of death turning into life.
        I am all of that.

I am the arroyo
        carved by wind
        and stories of time
        exposing tree limbs.
        I am those stories.
        can you hear me?

I am the bones
        I am the red
        I am the blood
        I am.
        I am river, far away
        I am the otter, gone today
        I am mine and minerals
        and pollution.
        I am toxic.
        earth is toxic.
        My body knows this.

I am eel, snake, cat, panther and amazon.
        I am cocoa bean and corn
        I am genetically modified.
        I am traditions dying
        I am grief, crying.
        I am cloud and mind drifting
        trying to escape to neverland.
        and I am roots, helping me to stay.

I am juniper, sage and stone
        I am a desert longing for words
        I am a desert longing for meaning.
        i am a desert longing for water.
        I am dry cracked, aging pottery.
        I am turquoise.
        I am coyote licking sky with primal screams.
        I am gourd, yucca. I am mullein growing
        in concrete wastelands singing a song about regeneration.
        I am soft, a rosette, candle rod, Jupiter candlestick.

I am remembering.
    I am.
    I am night, remembering
    dancing daydreams blackened.
    I am heat.
    I am cricket
    I am song
    I am.
    I am body. I am breast. I am tongue. I am sweat.
    I am age
    I am transitioning
    a leaf yellowing, curling, browning
    falling.
    I am summer flowers turning away from the sun.

I am birds migrating
    polar bears confused
    ice melting.
    I am wind. speeding, destroying, screaming, tearing.
    I am wake up.
    I am scare.
    I am fear.
    I am everywhere.
    restriction, oppression, hate and crime
    I am that too.

I am a sheep on a hillside
    a farmer in a field
    a raven on a white-washed picket fence.
    I am limbs.
    I am emotion.
    I am life I am.
    I am death too.
    and sorrow
    and grandfather hands.
    I am raining tears on forgotten lands

I am shouting to the full moon
  that I am pregnant too.
  I am pelvis and thighs
  and interconnectivity.
  I am truth and lies and electricity.
  I am tooth and nail, and skin and hair.
  I am page and I am pen.
  I am voice I am.

I am sleeping with frogs in murky ponds.
  I am making love to beetles beneath sun.
  I am a mosquito drawing blood.
  I am scratch.
  I am ant.
  I am termite, keeping the ecosystem alive.
  I am beginning all over again
  because I am fog
  before rain and after a long, dry day.
  I am willow dangling.
  I am now. I am tomorrow. I am yesterday.
  I am tired.

I am going to sleep
  again
  so that I shall wake up again
  and discover that I am again and again and again.

It happened like this

On open space there is a lake.
I went there just past the crescent of dawn.
To the east, across the road
the sky was gold
and to the West
the mountains were pink.
You know how it is when
you blush from really being seen. Only it wasn't shy.
More to do about being met
by a sun burning hard through clouds too vulnerable to say no.
It was like that.

The lake was ice. Blue ice.
The kind of blue that reminds you
of the moment night comes gently and
the moment night slinks, seductively, away.

I heard the ducks before I saw them
in the wetlands. Where it is brown and soft
and where the water is alive in tiny bursts. I felt jealous
of a language I cannot speak. I tried to decipher
the cacophony of quacks and
how many and what pitch and is this a morning song?
Or are they upset because their bottoms are cold?
Or because I'm spying on them?
I have no clue. Do you?

I kept goin'. Around the south side of Coot Lake.
Past the watercolor owls and the poem by Wendell Berry
about how walking with a lantern in the night,
teaches light. To know the dark, walk in the dark.

But the day was becoming itself
and I already know the night blooms.
I thought of coyotes. And the song of night.

The ducks were gossiping. I was still jealous.
I'm not yet intimate with
the language of ducks at dawn.
It seemed foolish. But I said goodbye to them.
 They got silent.
I cried. Because the silent morning
touched me without asking. I liked it.

The light was now exploding
between the east and the west
and I felt like a school girl's ping pong ball
boinging in between walls.
Sky was a language beyond gold. Mountains were a naughty pink.
It was, plainly put, sexy.

Got me thinking about love.
Suddenly they lifted.
Without notice.
Love is strange that way.
One hundred and forty seven was my guess.
Honking me awake. Singing?
Do geese shout? What the heck were they saying?
I want to understand!

All I know is that they were ecstatic, or so it seemed
…and it was…I lost everything…I lost my words…
good morning?…
 …*awesome* was the best I could come up with.

I rang out my tears. Directly into it.
Wild geese.
One hundred and forty seven. Or so
straight over my head.
Low...becoming a ...virtuous V.
And then it came to me.
The language of Love. Commanding me towards it.
Rushing, gushing over me. Lifting,
away, away.
Leaving me open in wide open space.
        And that's how it happened.

19

a cold poem

You wake restless.
It isn't the log
by the door that says,
"Put me
in the embers
and blow."

It isn't the wind
slamming
against the thin glass
of a summer cabin,
tempting you to stay
in the womb of wool
blankets six inches thick.

It isn't your bladder
demanding to be emptied
or your dog
muttering his simple dreams out loud.

You listen to the wind
from your warm, safe place
and rebel hard against it.
You listen to your bladder
and then the still wood.
You do what they say
in a familiar, dusty dark
that doesn't ask you
to think too much.

Nine steps to the door
feeling the walls only once,
you put on your hat
and your boots
and go, focused —
a once-forgotten arrow,
straight beyond the crooked roof
of the old tool shed
and the deep brown knobs
of white dancing Aspens,
landing naked and raw
in the open pasture.

You feel a story
 you cannot hear
on rural land at night
three stars scream
orion's belt tightens
The cold wind pushes
and pulls against
the slow rising heat
of a spine uncertain
if it should expand or contract.

You feel a story
 you cannot hear
on rural land at night

as three

  stars   scream bright

from Orion's strong, protected belt.

just a hearth

place: old US 2
bayfield county. eileen township.
norweigan settlement village
the golden fleece.
temp: minus thirty below.

late afternoon: throw a log on the fire.
go for walk on hard, white earth
on frozen lake and back to frozen dirt.
cracked lips. where are my fingertips?
icy wind steals feeling in thighs.

crow. gothic ice. tiny bubbles, white veins and lines.
simple fishermen in tin huts
"ya, eh?'"over cookie cutter holes.
and tall lumberjacks with plaid shirts
wearing thick beards with crystallized stars.

early evening: beneath the pines
a tiny iron hearth in a dark oak cabin
and split wood. only sixty bucks to keep warm all winter.
and the small axe with a red rusty handle.

sunset: hot breath on minus zero air.
throw a log on the fire. listen to owls. eat leftovers.
climb the loft and go to bed.
midnight: throw another log in the stove.
just before dawn: throw another log in the stove.
gray yellow air crisp and alive.

dawn: pee on snow.
put two buckets on the blue sled. walk to water house.
do not slip on ice. fill buckets with fresh water.
haul it.
and stop to notice things.
black acorns on ash smudged snow.
barbed wire and wild horses in the bright antique fields.
i like the way water sloshes on wool army pants
making instant popsicles on knees.

noon: nourish body
brown rice and burdock
and sesame and venison meat.
rest. throw another log on fire. listen.
blow flames with breath. write. make tea. smile to ghosts.
walk. find spine bones whiter than snow.

afternoon: hard, white earth
frozen lake frozen dirt
gratitude for simple things. haul water. chop wood.
my favorites: gather branches from old oak trees
and paper skin birch.
listen for owls. talk to crow. spy a fox.
throw another log on the hearth.

II. Womblines

the birds and the bees

slit earth
spine before time
before legs, before crawl
slither to slither
and belly to clay.

it is springtime
you know how it comes
subtly
don't be fooled.
time is
sun fish
 flashing
quickening
diving into waters deep
and rising swift
bones exposed

biology says
birds and the bees it's a springtime thing
he says sweat
and she says purr
he says yeow
and she says yes
and it fuses
the two
into the one
they speak without words sometimes.
nature in her winter cage
changes. a door opens. just like that.
it explodes.

and there is shedding
don't forget that orgasm implies
killing each other with pleasure
don't forget to let go
of what you know

she screams and
he howls and they
the one
become two
and the body reintroduces
primal to primal
belly brain to belly brain
words can die too
thank the body for what is true

did you know that the cold
earth is warming
across thighs
between mossy valleys
and every single phallic symbol
reaches higher to the moon?

she likes the springtime push
of seeds
a lot!
she likes the manic burst
of new shoots through earth
she is earth body now
and words are new buds
containing force

to be alive now is to be every cell exploding awake
yes i am
says that tall tree standing taller
she likes
the way he panthers into her
and prowls
his way
home to her night
at dawn. yes. this is good.

she likes waking to the sound of
his beast.
she likes the way
it rips the flesh from her spine
the scent of hair
the pinch of nails
the yes of push
 yes, she likes this too. don't you?

don't be afraid: be terrified
of honesty wilded
and broken open
she wonders what shall become of them
come summertime.
what kind of tree
will it flower or fruit and
what will it smell like when it blooms

spring says
surrender and push
 rise and fall to meet it
let it teach you
the truth about the birds and the bees

ode to passion

brutal sea. brutal moon. brutal waves.
and brutal foam birthing bubbles
dissolving on stones.
brutality is misunderstood.

you swell. so does the sea. the moon rises, falls
and eats itself in less than 30 days.
every night eats an entire day without feeling guilt.

passion. you teach yes and no
and now. Now!
and the rough edges of
grind, pulverize and
annihilate

and the soft, moist center of
the space between words

passion. you who are terrify and strip
vulnerability and willing
expose and explosion
and convulsions of creatures denied at birth,
thrown unconsciously
and unselfconsciously
upon gritty sand
while foam and wave slosh and slur.

there is no duality within the sea.
admit it:
you are hungry for the ocean's violent birth.
you have an addiction for Aphrodite's
delicious thighs born from testicle foam
upon ancient stories
of men and civilizations and sacrificial
gods rising and falling
again and again
and again.

oh pilgrim of passion!
remember this when you feel afraid:
regeneration will never kill what is essential
you cannot hold on

water is going to slide
 through your fingers.
   the waves naturally shove you
to your place.

passion does not wear spectacles.
nor does she
send out a formal invitation
with perfectly engraved letters.

passion inhales
she will crack you open
like a hazelnut

day and stars are born because of this.

the raising of the dead.

four dusky volcano seeds
dreaming of power
simmer little fruits
teach the hungry veins

smell: sticky red perfume of sin and
death and before
life.   feel: blood molting into love blue
feather beads and cool silver pools

listen: clouds colliding from winter into
spring. soft. hard! Ccash!
surrender: open your eyes
the earth anticipates mud for a reason

breathe: animals breathing mysterious secrets
primal body below below where
the heart thump thump below below
and body seeks body. heat and skin upon skin

droplets of lust juice aged
since fall descending into time
falling time into gravity falling
weightless. into more than   winter's weight

be careful. seasons season soul seeds
while thighs and caves hibernate growls
deep. deep blue black depth of depth
it is dangerous to travel beneath

ancient rift: man   woman
 someone wise separated sky from earth
naked is this truth. yet mountains
mountains quiver or sunset pink blush at dawn.

Hades took Persephone once only
once   he took her to the cool dark
center. once there she ate juicy jewels
they seeded into her. perennial seeds of return.

she is   despite her frustrated screams
his balm. his tempering chrysalis.
balance. earth rumble rumble tumble
emerging. moles once blind to light

bones rattle. hearts pop. below ribs
night screams with delight against the sun
she comes. he comes
undone.   this oh my god fruit

spilling down the chin
fight fuels fuck fuels fierce
liquid rebirth: spring comes.
cocoons: empty in their own timing

Becoming Mama

I am more than one body.
Not quite two,
but not one.

Mother.
Becoming mother.

My body is still mine for one month
and then it becomes food.
Shelter. Home. Attachment. Bonding.
Animal body mother body
belly to belly human *creatura* intelligence.
My body will not be mine.
It will be claimed by a little
suckling human animal.
She will claim my breasts.
Her hunger and power is fierce.
She grew me into more than one.

Mother. Mama. Mamacita.
Momma. Mommy. Mom. Mamachka.
Mat'. Mater. Mutter. Mum.
Mummy. Motherline. Ma.

Woman opens.
A new being comes out.
A story breaks in two. It does hurt.
And there is bliss. A new story
breathes from waters of life.

My bloodline
roots to the Italian Mama
the German Mutter
the Romanian and Hungarian
Mama and Anya
and the Russian-Ukrainian,
Mat'.

Matryoshka doll: originally
mother of big peasant family
healthy portly figure.

Ma: Etymology, 15th century.
Natural sound in baby-talk
imitative of sound made while sucking

In the recent dreamtime
my breasts were overflowing with milk.
Frothy bubbles.
Sweet, creamy sustenance. Flowing.
Does this make me a mother?

When I was an infant
I did not drink this.
I suckled on plastic.
Is a bottle a mother?
Later in the day, I mentioned the dream to my
midwife. "You should squeeze your nipples
to see if you have produced
colostrum. I bet you have."
I squeezed...
colostrum came out —just a wee bit.
my nipples, a shower of life.

33

My blood and fluids
will transform into milk.
My breasts are becoming a mother.
Weepy I was later in the day
because this is a miracle. My body is a miracle.
And it is normal.

I'm on the edge of a tribe of women.
A club I didn't belong to earlier,
inviting me to step
over the bridge from where I came. Their names are
mama. mother. mom.
When you see me in a month, you'll say, "there's another mama."

The birth
   of each mama is
         as miraculous as
the birth   of each baby.

I was mothering
myself
before becoming a mama.
I barely tasted this word.
I thought I had.
The word tastes distinctly different
inside the mouth of daughter.
I was not a mama then.   Animal mama body
is different than non-
         mama animal body.
               Body does not lie.

My body
is becoming anonymous.
          breasts.   belly.   round.   soft.
It will smell perfect to my baby.
She will know me by scent and taste
before she knows me by sight.
 I am
becoming richer. deeper. wider. fuller. rounder.
more than.

Every day,
my sweet lover
tells me I am beautiful.   He says,
"for 37 years you were not a
mama. and now you are becoming a
mama. it is so beautiful to witness."
As far as he is concerned, he was a
virgin before he made love to a pregnant
woman. Now he is also more than one.
We are more than two. Becoming
a family.

He tells me
she will love me more
 than i have ever known love.
more than anyone has ever
loved me. She'll look at me with eyes that are
already a universe.

I say that to become a
mama is to become more than
love. I know it will be difficult
too. I'm not romanticizing anything. There is
truth and simplicity to the sweetness. It is
healthy to be simple and sweet. Like the
milk i will make. I go
slowly and quietly through this last month so I can
hear and taste the sweetness more fully in my
mouth before speaking.

Mila's poppy

It was natural.
I don't care
what the midwives
or the homebirth circles
say.
I say: c-section
is natural too
Go ahead and challenge me.

Sure. I felt a lot of grief
because it didn't
go the way I wanted

I wanted the
*breathe-and-dance-and-groan-and-scream-and-moan-und-purr-and-yell-
and-yank-and-push-and-pull-and-sweat-and-ebb-and-flow-and-
completely-surrendered-to-the-ocean-and-to-the-moon-at-home-birth*
that
my mother
and her mother
did not experience.

I wanted
to give birth to
a new story.
The **powerofthebirthingbody** story
I thought and felt that power was taken
from my birthing body

During my birth story
I embodied fear
I rattled my bones in fear
and Mila marinated in my fear.
I believed what I believed:
that c-section was unnatural
and cut off from the 'way it should be'

Well guess what?
I'm taking it all back
right now
see this:

C SECTION is NATURAL
for Mila and me

Think about it:
every time I grieve my birth story
for not being 'natural'
I tell Mila that it was unnatural
and that she was born less than.
If I do this she will feel I'm sad
because she is here
and that I'm sad for her birthstory.
This story isn't true.

Mila doesn't know any birth story other than her own
and I cannot compare
the birth of an apple from a blossom
to the birth of an oak from an acorn
I just can't. and I can't compare
the birth of mila
to the birth of fill-in-the-blank's homebirth.

To compare
is to cut
off and
split.
Mila, I'm not giving you the splits.
I'm giving you the whole truth right now:
I am proud of your birth story sweet little star

Mila
I like that you came through my poppy belly
you know,
the belly with the poppy tattoo
the one that stretched and grew with you.
The one I got one or two days
after you were conceived
not knowing you were conceived.
I like that there is a scar now
that goes across my groin
just beneath my fat
through a poppy flower.

You came out of a magical transforming poppy,
you did!
That poppy was placed there strategically
with joy and pregnancy in mind.
It was put there to honor the story of grief
from an abortion ago ago ago
and to birth beauty
out of pain and regret.

Your heart was born deep inside mama's poppy belly
and here you grew and slept and ate
and sucked your foot.
You kicked and pushed against mama's poppy.
So it is no wonder
you should pick mama's magical poppy
as your doorway into this world.

Mila!
I like your birth story a lot!
I love that you are here!
I am beyond joyful that you are here!

You can tell your friends
after you are all grown up
that you chose to come out
of mama's poppy belly
and that you chose
to be frank breech.

You determined the course of your life
through the story of your birth
and what is unnatural to some
is quite natural to you.

You gave this mama
the gift of wholeness
when her poppy belly was split open wide
and you were yanked out!
I'm giving wholeness back to you now
and I want you to carry it until you die.

Do you know how many people
in this country
pay lots of dollars to 'heal'
from the wounds of their birth stories?
you don't need to ever do that.

Sweet precious poppy daughter
I'm proud of how you came into this world.

I love you
more than the soft white changeability of the moon
I love you
brighter than the intensity of the sun
and I love you
redder and more delicate
but just as fiercely open
as the poppies in the field.

Becoming mama II

I breathe, dream and wake
towards Mila.
Her face changes every day.
I see my grandma in her
and Tony's grandma
and Tony
and me.
But she is distinctly Mila
tho I'm not yet sure what that means

She is becoming Mila
 I am becoming mama
 Tony is becoming papa

I want to write about how juicy it is to become mama
it is tender and beautiful and sweet and soft
 but it is also a painful
rite of passage into adulthood.
Becoming mama is to wake up
brighter and brighter
and to mature.

It hurts to become mama.
My left breast hurts.
I don't get to sleep as much
I sleep with one eye open
tracking
listening
learning.
Mama brain is reorganizing.
Biologically, my brain is different than it was before.

It takes time to adjust to becoming food
and to having baby in arms most of day
snuggling on body
clinging to breasts, nursing
crying in ear.

I love this baby belly next to mama belly
this baby sweet smell in my nostrils
waking next to baby at night
breasts heavy with milk and hot from heat
and baby making gremlin sounds when she first starts to eat.
I like this baby gremlin of mine
this baby creatura.

My body head arms forearms pelvis still healing
 from c-section aches
from rocking
bouncing holding
swinging shooshing
bouncing holding
rocking loving

It hurts to love this much.
She cracks me open several times a day
with her inconsolable cries
and her big eyes
and her 'you mean i left the womb for this' look of horror
her cheek against my gigantic breast
her breathing deep and soft as she falls asleep.

This Mila baby is growing fast
she furrows her brow a lot
and cries tiger cries
and whimper cries
and cooing cries
and sleepy cries
and escape from the swaddle cries
and give me more milk cries

and she loves me with
tiger baby love snarls
and koala baby love cuddles
and furry rabbit love snuggles
and tiny kitten love nursing
and sweet smelling baby love

Seula

Our wombs are sleeping together.
Their wombs breathe together.
 They blow foam to the shore together.
 They sing a mnemonic song.
Seula. Seula. Seula.
Not with their mouths or the minds.
 Their song is deeper than time.
Their song is embedded in stone before words were what we now
know.
 Their song carries symbol in pure form,
It takes time to follow and unravel.

Seula travels through my German bloodine.
Old Germanic soul
 from womb to womb
 life to death to life
to return.
It aches when I call it forth.
They say it comes from the root
'to bind'
and the ancient practice of
binding the corpse
after death
to prevent the soul from returning.

My father's fatherline
and my mother's fatherline
tell me it is of the breath.
Anima. Psyche. Soul. Dusha.
Dusha. Butterfly. Psyche. Anima.

Last week I met a whale for the first time.
I was with Mila. We were gathering
unbroken sand dollars.
A salty red-headed fisherman
pointed and said, 'Hey, see that?'
It was the one day I didn't bring my glasses
because I had given up on seeing whales.
Does that mean I had given up on soul?

I'd been searching, straining my eyes
on daily morning walks with Mila
beyond waves and headlands
praying, 'please please please
may I see a whale today.'

I dreamed of them when they were passing through —
heading towards Mexico.
A pod of whales swimming
beneath the surface singing
and I awoke thinking
how I rarely dream
of animals.
The dream was medicine. A secret
 buried treasure. It felt
as rare as glimpsing a whale
from a beach.
A part of me didn't trust whales
or that they really exist.
Yet my dreaming mind wanted me to know:
 there is much more happening below the surface
of what I think I see and know and believe.

So it was thrilling
ecstatic even, to see one so close
to where Mila and I gathered sand dollars.
I mean, I could have jumped into the water
and swam right out to touch his tail.
The waves rolled soft and gently
and he was playing.
He was little, his tail was big.
And he blew air
shaped like hearts
again and again and again.

Sand dollar. Blue whale. Fisherman.
 *H*eart. Seula. Splash. Sand dollar.
Blue whale.

It caught me loudly in my chest
 when the second whale emerged
bigger, further in the distance.
I imagined, she was his mama.

That night
I dreamed again of their song.
This time, the pod was closer
and a medicine man was on the shore translating for them
I didn't need a translator.
I was mesmerized by how it felt
and the knowing it touched deep in the belly.
It was the way a homecoming feels
when your longing brings you back
 to where you came from
even though you've been changed
a hundred times from caterpillar to butterfly to egg
 to caterpillar.
It sounded like a prayer
And it felt like an orgasm.
Not the kind that comes from sex.
It vibrated through me. It was creation
singing me awake
unraveling that which had been bound.
my longing for her was fierce.

III. Re-wilding

untitled

rustic
new language.
simplicity among rhododendron, fern.
engaged to salt
to wave.
octopus dreams and i am
body ecosystem.
sensual. rugged. moist. soft. greening.
delighting in eucalyptus
and forest crow atop usnea bearded pines

peeing on bushes beneath star & milky way
way, way beyond what is civil.

pioneering with hummingbird
i am becoming this whale song
mnemonic memory lulling my sleep
dreaming water dreaming me dissolving into
womb time
my baby, my lover
we are simplifying.

beneath beneath

going into underground
willingly.
allergic to surface.
depth. i want depth.

i like the places where
meaning is more than.
you have to travel beneath language
in order to get it.

you have to travel beneath
beneath what you think you know
and what you think you see

i like this.
and the way the worms
give and take from the soil.
it is important to be seasoned by unassuming
and simple thing.

i like the hidden stories
beneath night
and dawn
and breath.

i miss walking upside down.
in summer when things fly above above
and grief is evaporated by clouds
my pelvis aches.
 my mind doesn't know it.

beneath is a season.
it grows me more
than the insouciance of butterflies.
it may seem strange,
but i prefer the worms that curl their forms round decay
and turn death into new life.

Demeter can tend the harvest above.
i need the below and her stories
descending into my skin.

now is the time
to crawl naked to belly clay
in primal time; mud and earth
its own song caked to flesh
yes! please! yes!

thighs thundering YES
beneath beneath
 depth
where beneath becomes something else
something not yet a word
forming into more than.

Re-enchanting Erotic

sea anemone floating over dunes.
body against tree
rough bark fingers reading bark lines. tracing
bark lines on sand. plunging fingers
into sand through dry
 into wet. bark smell. is bark smelling me
 or am i smelling bark? we tangle tango
limb to limb moss earth puerrh taste in mouth.
sucking resin from pine needles.
bright tang awake in mouth
bitter and sticky and slightly sweet.

forever green is erotic. i want to be
forever green like the clitoris. clitoris
is the only body part that never ages.
forever green. timeless is erotic. floating
dreams. edo period. but here i am now
body on plastic chair writing
in building with sound of breadmachine
humping dough. i write towards the erotic.
escaping monotony hum hum hum buildings
to mossy moist mounds soft earth sinking
into earth where roots extend wide
 not deep beneath red wood. red wood is erotic.
redwood. beyond erection.
into sky where mind is clear
bright blue the color of eros.

i like contrasts.
eros sky. red clay. blue vein. red blood.
ocean wave. red soil. soil
is erotic. anything that grows
in or out of soil
is erotic. feet-bulbs
planted in mud simultaneously descending
and arching ascending. do you see trees dance?

i knew a man who smelled like cinnamon
embodied night. he was chocolate skin
spicy skin thick lips deep
root howls. on a nature walk
he asked me to get on my knees
put my head in a hollow trunk,
dig my hands in moist earth
inhale deep. trees started dancing after that.
roots transforming into snakes meandering
across my body the way fingers
meander across bark. leaf breathing
drinking 5 am dew. wet
unassuming wonders of the world. branches
whispering humidity against my back
against the banks of lake. nature is hot.
and cool. and deer antler soft. raven
chasing night
away swoosh swoosh velvet black caress.

a thousand trees frozen dancers
 in ecstasy. please look. at them this way.
don't be shy.
be shameless with them.
see feel know in body
pelvis limbs eyes heartbrainheart
there is no such thing as frozen.
sap rises. slowly up. slowly down.
descending ascending simultaneously. dancing.
mirroring movement of worms.
worms are erotic too.

i'm going to meander.
 i'm being pulled, tossed and shaken
fiercely towards ocean. because ocean
is erotic too. ocean wave spray fierce
shattering shell pulling back, back back pushing
forward. below below octopus
and whale and vibration
and shiny pink shell reflecting birth.
ocean. OSH UN! coming again rolling,
forcing me to lick her salt off my lips.

ocean
is more than wet
she salivates
for shore. that rock standing alone
 waiting for ocean to crash against it.
tell me that isn't erotic. redefining
force on force.

and then there is moon.
secret tidal wave opening
coaxing unwinding undulating
stories hidden inside stories
hidden inside body mostly in hips
pelvis thigh and womb and uterus
fallopian tubes connected to uterus
looks like butterfly inside is pink and shiny
and oh yeah, here we go again back to the beginning
yoni to shell to ocean to clitoris to ageless.
and that is erotic because i have it
and it drinks words through my skull
and images through my eyes.

Becoming Family

it didn't matter if i was married
or not
if i was with a man
or a woman
or a gorilla
or not.

seriously.

except that when tony and i met,
despite
or maybe because of,
a thousand and one differences,
i knew instantly:
he would be her papa.

unashamed, i asked
 the first time after we made love.
and he said
'er, um, don't you think it is a little soon
to be asking me
for my baby? let's
keep getting to know each other. for awhile!'
and then he gently added, 'i should be scared
but for some reason that doesn't freak
me out. i'm not running away'

sometimes you just know things
in your skin
despite how crazy
or illogical it seems.
for instance,
the day he helped me move my furniture
from my former home
to my new home on a farm
where he was one of several roommates i'd never before met
he felt like he was helping his girlfriend
and that we'd known one another
forever.

i typically do not like the word 'forever.'
it grows beyond my body
in a way that makes me
feel challenged to breathe.
the word: 'wife'
same sensation.

but mama...
i love being
mama
i don't need
or want
to be 'wife'
to be mama.
i'm kind of a shrew
and i am difficult to tame.
but, i am an amazing mama.
really. i was made for this miracle.

 the birth of something
changes you.
if you have kids, you know this.
if you don't, you still know it
babies really are different than creative projects
 there is a long tunnel bridge between where i am now
and where i was before i had a baby

where was i?
oh yeah..
i was, he was
we were
thirtysomethings
adventuring
fiercely independent. passionate. a little fickle about life.
and life purpose.
we squared one other. it was edgy. and intense.

i'm learning that two squares eventually rub
the edges into rounded and
 unusual shiny shapes.
just so you know: we aren't two halves
trying to make a whole. nah.
i used to love plato's idea —
about how human beings used to be joined together
two halves whole.

but they were always getting into trouble
so the creator split them apart and scattered them to separate ends
of the earth
to spend the rest of their lives
or lifetimes
searching
to be reunited
to that other half.

honestly,
i'm not sure i'll ever be a wife or a bride
i certainly don't want to be a missus
though we do fantasize about our
rednose clown wedding
and how we will surprise and delight
and shock our guests when
i run away from the altar. fast. screaming
into the woods and he and
his best men go running into the fields
with butterfly nets
to catch me

but this isn't about our eccentric
unconventional love or is it?
i honesty don't know what love is.
what is love? do you know?
since mila,
love is
new. young. immature in the language
 of spring plants. curious.
soft.
and squishy
and messy

57

sometimes stinky
it cries from its entire self
it experiences heightened joy
and sensation beyond star
and milkyway bright
i've never known love
to be so so small
and fragile
and permeable
and honest

it absorbs everything.
this thing called love
will grow strong
and bountiful
and confident
and wise with deep roots
and wide branches
and it is honest.

i am digging my toes inside of it
growing a garden is not cliche.
it is necessary to sustain my belly.
love sustains my belly
and it squeezes oceans out of my eyes

damn. love is
HUGE
and so small in the same breath
how can something so big
pass through such a tiny opening?
in my case,
surgeon baba yaga
cut open and pulled love
out of my belly
it was upside down.
feet first

where am i going?
you already know
i am becoming a mama
and tony is becoming a papa
and mila is
365 days out of the belly
becoming ONE
and we are birthing a family
three inside of one hearth

in an upside down
create it as you go
choose your own adventure
book of love

MOLT

Scorpions have many eyes but do not see well. They feel their way through dark and sense light through shadow with sensory hairs. They glow at night. They can live up to 25 years of age and go a year without eating. Their mating battle dance can last up to 18 hours. They will sting one another intentionally. Males run away from females after mating to avoid post-coitus, cannibalistic inclinations. They' are wise. They've been around for 430 million years. And once had gills.

Scorpion mamas are fierce mamas. They keep their young on their backs until the babes fall off and are ready to hunt for themselves. While wearing my babe on my back, I tapped into mamaprotector ferocity after discovering a scorpion on the floor ready to crawl into a pair of Mila's socks. The scorpion invited me into her ancient, dusty, slow metabolic dream. She is archaic messenger between the worlds. Midwife and psychopomp of soul. She pointed her stinger at my attention and raised the vibration of electricity in my heart.

Stinger on, pedipalps ready for battle, I scooped her up off the floor with a jar. Fear rattled my belly and bones. The transformative power of fear. The kind that tastes like excitement but lives in a word not yet invented because it breathes beneath listening, inside listening, inside just-after-death and just-before-birth. The raw energy felt like the heartbeat drum beat boom-boom of revolutionary evolution. The kind of boom boom that beats poison into ego resisting yet screaming for change. Sting the status quo! Sting the things you wish to fling! Her stinger forced me to shut up and listen. Listen through belly –hers and mine – beneath vibration of sound beyond a dozen eyes to sensing of light within dark.

She asked: What are you afraid of? What do you need to let go of? What are you willing to sting within yourself and annihilate so you can give birth to a new form? Do it. Molt, girlfriend, molt. And they molt. Many times in a lifetime. Molt, woman, molt. Annihilate the old, babe. Annihilate everything that doesn't serve. Crawl on earth from your belly. Feel your way through dark. Feel your truth and let it lead you. Annihilate the lies and delusions. Go straight to the center. To the raw naked shivering soul catalyzing itself into a new story.

Baubo

I'm so on the surface.
I grow and grow and
I'm feeling muddy and ruddy.
red earth. From the belly
to the belly. Clay and jungle bugs
and mystery and awakening.
Juice. From the fruits. Of the trees. And the sounds at night
of snakes and animals delighting in moonlight frolicking.
I am your sin.

Come closer girl.
shto devushka....ya tozhe baba yaga!
what girl? I am also Baba Yaga!
I will eat you if you get close, yes,
that's right, close, closer.
Step out of the light. Down under
into the sun of oblivion and earth
where it is hot and fiery
and legs grow trunks into sky.
Dance, girl, dance and let yourself fly.

That's right. Go. Grow. Growl.
Get out of the rut.
Rut with your man.
Rut with your stuff.
strut and rut and cock a doodle doo!
That's right. It's crazy here, that's right.
Yup, that's right. What do you know, girl,
What do you know? You know,
Where you feel it, down there
where it is hot and ripe and
Juicky and alive. Yes, Juice-ky.
Invent words, girl.

Get out of your own way lady!
Come on, I am talking to you too.
Now that I have your attention,
what do you want to do?
dance and sing and laugh
and make mirth.
myth and mirth. that's write, girl. right?

Ah huh, that's how it goes,
That's how it grows.
too bad for the caterpillar in its cocoon.
Don't know if someone's gonna eat you.
Don't know what you are gonna turn out to be.
Don't know if you will fly.
You might just keep on
dissolvin'.
Dissolvin. for the love of God,
dissolve some more, will ya?
keep drippin' your stuff, capiche?
Ecco lo! E juisto.Sono anche Strega Nonna.
eh, that's right. I'm Strega Nonna too. Mangia Mangia
Eat-ah your words-ah! And eat-ah some more-ah!

(you want-ah more-ah? I know you do...
Jungle dance and jungle swim.
Jungle monkey and jungle baby. jungle honey.
Jungley jungle bungle of a bungle
of a jungle of a mother red earth
What?
 What the ... *Chort Vozmi!*
What and where
and why?

Stip stop. trip trop. Hop. bop.
bippity boppity boo.
You do believe in magic don't you?
Well, get on witht then. Go. Step right up. Step right up!
Here we go again. Around and around
and around she goes, where she stops nobody knows......

here I am in the wheel,
yes I am
and it is turning
and I am riding
and spinning
and down under there is fierce light
 bubbling, brewing, offering
tempting me, drowning me
drinking me, becoming me.
light.
into light I fly.

I am heat and sky and heart blazing ensouling
skin with leopard print of steadfast courage
awake to sun
it is time to run
seduced by jungle aromas
and cawcaws
and macaws
and paws
and yes,
get out of your own way girl!
That is what I said.

If you remember only one thing it is this and I say it again
Get out of your own way!
Dance!
Fly and stop lyin'
Stop tryin'
Be what you came here to be. Simply put.
Who is that, girl?
Oh wait, you aren't a girl.
What are you then?
oh, caterpillar…
no wait…
butterfly, is it you?

Now I see you!
So what are you waiting for?
What are you afraid of?
What keeps you bound?
Fly and fly and fly to sky to the
moon! Howl and then
rip it off! Tear it off
Cut it off! Growl it off!
Shuck it off! Dance it off
Asunder. Hot fiery red spice
Yum. Passion in oblivion
keep grinding

Gyrating. Pounding
Gripping. Exploring
Exploding plums
against the sun
Fucking hot
red hot cinnamon
sin sin city
come on
come on feel the noise
oh boy. come on Eileen
come on boys
come on, come one come all
Come alive
yes! Don't be shy
Scream it! Paint it on the sky
I AM ALIVE!

Call to Adventure

I want to tell you about
how juicy my heart is
for my baby daughter *creatura*.

It's like when you eat a summer peach
you know —that first bite —
and the next and the juice so sweet and sticky
and the way it drips down your hands
and your lips and your chin
and it is sensual and innocent
in the same breath
and you like it
so much you have to eat
the rest very very slowly

It is both innocent and sensual to be a mama.
I love it.

Since becoming *mamacreatura*
I WANT TO TRAVEL
for the rest of my life.

I need to live in a hut
that wanders on chicken feet through forests
and caves and meadows and deserts and
I want to ride a cauldron
across several different oceans.

I need to see
and stay and see.
I said that on purpose because once
I lived with an Indian family
in London. The girl I cared for had 14 servants in India.
Even one to wipe her butt.
I was her one and only American nanny.
But anyway, her grandfather told me
that my name, Stacey, means
"If you stay, you shall see."

He said it was a good name.
After I write this poem,
I will start growing into my name.

I need a new feeling —the kind
when you go to a city you've never been to
like Moscow, Russia
and you have an uncanny way of navigating
as if you lived there
once, long, long ago.

For starters, I need to see
Sicily. No, it would be more accurate to say:

I want to make love to Sicily.
I want to crawl through a Mongolian Steppe.
Kiss Tibetan stones.
Laugh in a Kazakhstani market and
feast forever in the country of Georgia.
Listen to a violin in Albania!
Dance on Transylvania and Romania!

I want to walk on an Irish cliff
and pounce on a fairy mound.
I want to go to places. and Stay and See.

Place me on the map and let me fly.

I need to meet the people
who live in places.
I need to hear their stories.
Because it is how I grow.
It is how I learn.
It is how I become less of what I was
and more of what I want to be.

I spent $24,000 a year on undergraduate education
And the ONLY thing that made sense
Was 10 months in Moscow.
During a Revolution. Everything opened.
My eyes were Glasnost, my heart a big fat Perestroika.

This is my spirituality.
And it is devoid of sparkles. It wants roots and
Place and Nomads and Archetypal Gypsies. Root stories.
Worn soles. Warm souls. Exchanging
stories. From the belly. Over tea & saurkraut.

This is what I want more of:
to travel
to see
to unlearn
and to return
changed.

I want to carry my baby daughtercreatura butterbottom
across the ocean
to islands and countries and Places
so we can dance inside of new languages.

I get turned on
By exotic foreign wordbirds
flying through my sleep
opening my eyes awake to life.

I like the life
of sensing through
Place. I want to taste breathe
suck eat drink fuck it
Yes, that is what I wrote.
And so, I will plant this poem like an acorn in the ground
and stomp around in circles all over it
and mark a big enough space for it to grow a traveling fairytale
wonderland adventureland forest of stories.

Call to Adventure (reprise)

I need to catch stories
from faraway lands
and eat them.
I need to feed foreign stories
 to my family too.

The call to adventure
Is screaming and I am dreaming
of flying with shamans.
Last night in the dreamtime
I pulled myself out of
a wormhole.
It was cold and sludgy and
I remembered:
I know how to fly.
It isn't like riding a bicycle.
Gravity can be an anchor
and doubt – lumpy stones in my skin.

Dream-flying is born in my thighs
where strength roots.
It speaks the language of monarchs awakening
and quickens a fierce lightness in me.
I defy myself. I fly.
When I try, I fall. It has to be
a leap
beyond belief
through faith and straight into the cellular memory
of butterflies and imaginal buds activated
during dissolution.
I have imaginal buds too.
Caterpillars work hard.
Butterflies just are.

It was hot in my bed when I awoke
The fireplace was a supernova
and we were all tossing and turning.
Mila couldn't stop giggling –

first while nursing, then standing up
at the head of our bed and spontaneously
flinging her little monkeybody with all her might
onto softness. Squeaking joy
as if saying, "gravity is fun, mama. gravity too is fun."

I want to fling myself into the unknown
and land joyfully inside a south American rainforest
where I can make love to the smell of orchids
slosh my bare feet in red clay
harvest mate leaves, drink them from a bombilla
and watch Mila run after
blinking iridescent wings
By summer I want to exchange root stories
and winged stories
with an international tribe of nomads and archetypal gypsies.
We'll recognize one another by our warm souls
and happy soles on mushy, rich soil.

Here sits my equinox & Aries new moon
prayer: May I live my life as a poem,
spin cocoons inside new languages
and emerge from them changed.
May I discover a corn-filled rattle in my dreams tonight
shake these words into the sky
and watch as they sprinkle the ground
like cacao pods. May the sun roast them mighty good.
I'll jump on them, crack them open
and eat them the way a caterpillar devours itself.
They will grow an unconventionally wild family tree
from our bellies and through exotic story forests
with roots that journey deep into the heart
of unknown territories and ordinary magic.

What Spring Said

Spring ain't the time for lettin' go. That's winter's job.

Spring seeds want you to get aggressive. Are you feelin' the pressure? Good! Dig deep w/ your feet but reach higher for sun. Have healthy conflict. Without pussyfooting around. It might be messy. It's part of nature. Normalize it. Allow your ego to breathe and express itself. Stop being afraid of or diminishing the awesome power of your ego. Without it, you wouldn't have purpose, so let it shine! Be fierce and resurrect something. Stop saying sorry. Stop feeling bad. Stop worrying. Stop being afraid. Lose your faith for forty nights if you want, and then find it with a passion that would make Jesus envious. Tell someone how you really feel. Be honest. Be real. Learn from your Aries pals. Boldly go where no one has gone before. Butt your head into something and don't apologize. Butt your head into something again. And again. Climb a mountain sideways like a ram, not straight up like a goat. Don't worry about getting to the top.

Rock the babe w/ sass. Let her cry. Let yourself cry. And scream. And laugh. And fart. And belch. And make mistakes. And notice what new awkward thing you are re-learning this spring. Give yourself permission to do it with baby steps. Without feeling embarrassed. Be even messier without shame.

Make room for small explosions. Don't fear them.

If you want to suffer, suffer, but do it in style! Make it dramatic and give it flair. Have fun with it. Take it out on a date. Or dance with it in your living room. Make fun of where you take yourself too seriously. Stretch out the winter serious-ity. Pop if you need to. Poop if you need to. Jump if you need to. Skip if you need to. hop if you need to.   have sex if you need to. birds do it, bees do it. Don't apologize.

Stop trying, you are lying.
Just do it.
What explodes now will flower in june.
And harvest in fall.
And let go and sleep or transform in winter.

Spring isn't about letting go!

It's about pushing through!
push, push, push!
go on little seed!
and baby steps.
and mess.
and mud.
and erratic unpredictability
and impulse!
and ramming
and butting heads.
and conflict. Yes!

It's okay little seed, grow!
Don't be shy. Go for it!
come on little seed...

Sun's waiting for ya
wants 'ta shine on ya
wants to soak you through and through
with hot, bright, expansive, mind-blowing, brilliant, don't stare at it
or you'll go blind, light!

So forget about the snarlies
and the willies
of fall and winter
or the hoochies and the coochies from yesteryear

Embody yourself already! Whatever is nascent and new amidst the
clouds
focus on that!
make it bigger than big even if you are small
have a healthy attitude
the season makes the new seeds work pretty hard
against windy and extreme forces.
so what are you waiting for? Ready, set, go!

Waking Inside

It is a soft time to be between
awake and alive.
To greet the senses
of nature and body
slowly, sensuously

Later i'll return to this moment
to try and say it just so,
so that you understand how
the rose of dawn opened
and suspended me this morning
between verbs.

But she's left. And the blue is reaching, extending
past the boundaries that were visible
moments before.
Early blue sky: the briefest moment
a blushing cradle
now arms and limbs and breath stretching
becoming morning
shedding night.

We meet here beneath the blue
day after day after day
barely conscious of the journey we took
to awaken. I don't mean rise and shine.
i mean Rise and Shine.

It's easy to forget, neglect, become habituated to, take it for granted.
   this dawn. Dawn.
she. it. he?
How do you see it?
Does it depend on where you stand in relation to it?
Or did you already miss it?
Again? And again?

This spirited, creative intelligence
happens. To say happens
sounds trite.
But it happens. Dawn happens.
Over. And over and over.
Dawn crawls and rolls and turns and lifts
off the tail of it's former self.
Dawn happens.

Like the verb of night.

You say, night is a verb?
Yes.   Night is a verb.
It draws black things
over dreams and eyes.
Night happens.
Night happens!

But now.
let's talk about right now.
can you feel the reverberation
of stillness between owls' hooting?
It happens so fast. And it also suspends.
depending on where you stand
in relation to it.

The soul of my body aches for something,
someone to connect with on top of now.
The body wants you to remember
the way we bodies are meant to re-member things.

But I've already edited this
and now has passed.
I'll remind you of what now wants:
Now wants you to feel the tear of sky
just before it rips the blackness open –
just before it moistens
your skin
with salt and water –
just before it grows into the action of light.

But these words: night and day
change quickly
because day killed night again
and rose higher than the verb of dawn.
the owls have already flown towards it

leaving me with this poem,
a scrappy leftover.

Detours

The thing about detours is they always take you
where you want to go.

Just not the way you want.
So what?
Even if you have to inch along, crawl
at a slug's slow pace
you're going to get 'there'
and what's the problem with slugs anyway?
Have you ever witnessed the way they dance
or dangle from trees
and make love for hours and hours mid-air?
What must they be feeling? Surely they aren't thinking.
Surely, they know something about slow that we don't.

But we don't want to look at the slugs.
We want to rabbit our way down the road.
Bounce sprightly back and forth to the truth
Detour is part of the eco-system.
Detour and Transition, the ecology of our modern times
Getting lost and found
Forgetting and awakening.

Dante said
"In the middle of the journey of our life,
I came to myself, in a *selva obscura*
a dark wood,
where the direct way was lost.
It is a hard thing to speak of,
how wild, harsh and impenetrable that wood was,
so that thinking of it recreates the fear.
It is scarcely less bitter than death: but, in order to tell
of the good that I found there,
 I must tell of the other things I saw there."

Who else is in a *selva obscura*?
Raise your hand if you feel as if you've been on a detour!

Midlife isn't a simple dream.
Perhaps the world is in midlife too and we're just part of the
ecology
 of the dark woods
the collective ecology of lost and found
beasts and burdens
beauty and blossoms

Let's get archeological together
 and dig to the potato filled depths
and nourish ourselves with the soup made from roots
You wanna figure all of this out?

Grock this: The detour is part of the poem,
part of the dream
part of life
part of the road
part of the blocking, the block
part of getting from there to here
it's the in between part

that we are supposed to wake up inside of

even though we don't want to be in it
(or on it)

such a hassle anyway!

but dig deeper
to the roots
and the forgetting
will awaken

Grock this: Soul isn't discerning. A path, is
a path, is a path. Is a path.
Construction zone and all.
And the soul simply wants to know.
To experience. To quest. No questions,
no answers.

The soul wants to adventure..
Nothing ventured, nothing gained.
The soul wants to know Good
Bad. Evil. God. Light. Dark. Beast Sensation.
Pleasure. Pain. Numb. Comfort. Dis
comfort. Stuck. Un
stuck. The soul isn't discerning.
The ecology of soul isn't duality. It's
whole-ality. Totality.
And so, the path winds
and twists
and turns
through meadows hedges
brambles cities
thorny rose gardens
construction sites
nuclear war zones
genocidal horrors
dark forests
and ancient labyrinths.

I am, we are, you are a human being
on another fucking journey.
Lost, found, on a detour, lost again
returning and detouring and returning.
What if we are the wheels on the road?
The next time you find yourself hating
that you are on yet another metaphorical detour
remember, the divine is turning the wheels
down the bumpy detour-filled path.

the same way
 it turns sun and moon and stars.

www.ingramcontent.com/pod-product-compliance
Lightning Source LLC
LaVergne TN
LVHW011338080426
835513LV00006B/418